I'M A PARENT?

KNOCK KNOCK®
VENICE, CALIFORNIA

Created and published by Knock Knock
Distributed by Who's There Inc.
Venice, CA 90291
knockknockstuff.com

ISBN: 978-160106134-8
UPC: 825703-50024-0

20 19 18 17 16 15 14 13 12 11 10 9 8 7 6 5 4 3 2

PARENTING:
IT'S THE HARDEST JOB YOU'LL EVER HAVE.

It's a lifelong, 24/7 vocation where you're constantly on call, in crisis mode, and required to make executive decisions on everything from appropriate snack choices to prom-night curfews on the spot and without an instruction manual, all the while battling waves of fear, doubt, and regret. Who could blame you for feeling like you may (literally) lose your mind at the mere drop of a sippy cup?

Although it may seem like you're alone in a sea of hyper-competent, over-achieving, make-it-all-look-effortless "#1" moms and dads—you're not. For consolation, simply look to the countless television shows, memoirs, and blogs (not to mention Facebook posts) that give vent to the rather messy realities of family life and the omnipresent anxieties most parents feel about their child-rearing inadequacies. It's high time we all take a collective sigh of relief, and admit that the Cleaver model is outdated, impossible, and downright ridiculous.

Regardless of the progressive cultural climate, however, you're probably still struggling with the burden of responsibility that parenting heaps upon even the most prepared. Whether it's nature or nurture, it's *your* fault if your kids are screwed up—either by the genes that you've passed along or what (you have a sneaking suspicion) may be general incompetence. For everything you may be doing right (and there must be something), you could also be doing it very, very wrong. Are you giving your kids enough TLC or smothering them? Is discipline or leniency the most effective tactic? Are you producing spoiled brats or deprived ragamuffins?

These anxieties are a natural response to the most important obligation you will probably ever know. But they're not making our kids any happier. According to a survey conducted by the Families and Work Institute in New York, the most common wish of the children polled was for a less stressed out mom and dad. Your kids are going to be with you for a *long* while—the Society for Adolescent Medicine now puts the cutoff age between child and grown-up at twenty-six—so the sooner you learn to cope, the better.

Some modern parents have found catharsis (and remuneration, in the form of ad sales and book advances) by chronicling their tribulations in the blogosphere, bolstering themselves with comments from others who praise them for giving voice to the fears they too secretly harbor. However, those comment fields can be as pernicious as they are supportive. So how can you healthily manage chronic parenting unease without subjecting your fragile ego to flaming sanctimommies and daddies? The solution, thankfully, lies in your hands. Whether you feel overwhelmed and need a space where you can vent guilt-free or are happily imperfect and want to record your personal observations about child-rearing without fear of ridicule, a journal provides a private, nonjudgmental repository for your feelings.

Parenting authorities all agree that parents have it tough, and journaling is a cost- and time-efficient way to help them relax. The venerable Heidi Murkoff, author of the *What to Expect* series, advises new parents to "find a quiet spot, be honest, and let the words flow." In addition to helping to put one's mind at ease, journal writing has been shown to aid physical health as well. According to a widely cited study by James W. Pennebaker and Janel D. Seagal, "Writing about important personal experiences in an emotional way ... brings about improvements in mental and physical health." Proven benefits include better stress management, strengthened immune systems, fewer doctor visits, and improvement in chronic illnesses such as asthma. (Clearly, it's better to vent than to hyperventilate.) You don't need a medical license or a degree in child psychology to understand that healthier, happier people make better parents.

It's not entirely clear how journaling accomplishes all this. Catharsis is involved, but many also point to the value of organizing experiences into a coherent narrative. According to *Newsweek*, some experts believe that journaling "forces us to transform the ruminations cluttering our minds into coherent stories." Writing about an experience can help you distance yourself from the feelings of inadequacy that get in the way of enjoying the just-as-real joys of parenting. In many ways, journaling can be used as a panic-filter that enables the more rational side of us to take the reins.

As a devotee of this journal, you obviously have the self-awareness to take control of your feelings and self-worth. You may have doubts about your parenting skills, but you know it's smarter to work through them on paper, rather than let them fester into guilt (which your kids will later learn to take advantage of). But you also don't have time for purposeless navel-gazing or self-destructive wallowing. You want results. So here are a few tips to help you get the most out of journal writing.

Specialists agree that in order to reap the benefits of journaling you have to stick with it, quasi-daily, for as little as five minutes at a time, even on the days you are *not* struggling with pangs of guilt or barely concealed anger. Finding a regular writing time (rather than looking for a free moment) and a comfortable location (away from the kids) can help with consistency. If you find your busy mind suddenly drawing a blank just as you pick up the pen, don't stress. Instead, use the quotes inside this journal as a jumping-off point for observations and explorations. Write whatever comes to you, and don't criticize it; journaling is a process of self-reflection, not a structured composition. In other words, spew. Finally, determine a home for your journal where your child won't find it— such as in the health-food pantry.

Actor, comedian, and father Bill Cosby once said, "No matter how calmly you try to referee, parenting will eventually produce bizarre behavior, and I'm not talking about the kids." Take it from the man who played one of the most beloved father figures in television history: it's normal for things to get a little nutty. But before you know it, your doubts will turn to tried-and-true wisdom, and soon enough you'll have a book full of your own nuggets regarding the rewards of parenthood—not to mention pages of material to embarrass your kids with when they get a little older.

If you have never been hated by your child, you have never been a parent.

DATE		

WHY I'M A LESS-THAN-PERFECT PARENT TODAY:

_____
_____
_____
_____
_____
_____
_____
_____
_____
_____
_____
_____
_____
_____
_____
_____
_____
_____
_____
_____
_____
_____
_____
_____
_____
_____
_____
_____
_____
_____

TODAY'S PARENTAL SHORTCOMINGS INVOLVED:

Children are all foreigners.

RALPH WALDO EMERSON

DATE		

WHY I'M A LESS-THAN-PERFECT PARENT TODAY:

_____

_____

_____

_____

_____

_____

_____

_____

_____

_____

_____

_____

_____

_____

_____

_____

_____

_____

_____

_____

_____

_____

_____

_____

_____

_____

TODAY'S PARENTAL SHORTCOMINGS INVOLVED:

Any kid will run any errand
for you, if you ask at bedtime.

RED SKELTON

DATE		

WHY I'M A LESS-THAN-PERFECT PARENT TODAY:

_____

_____

_____

_____

_____

_____

_____

_____

_____

_____

_____

_____

_____

_____

_____

_____

_____

_____

_____

_____

_____

_____

_____

_____

_____

_____

TODAY'S PARENTAL SHORTCOMINGS INVOLVED:

In order to influence a child, one must be careful not to be that child's parent or grandparent.

DON MARQUIS

DATE		

WHY I'M A LESS-THAN-PERFECT PARENT TODAY:

_____
_____
_____
_____
_____
_____
_____
_____
_____
_____
_____
_____
_____
_____
_____
_____
_____
_____
_____
_____
_____
_____
_____
_____
_____
_____

TODAY'S PARENTAL SHORTCOMINGS INVOLVED:

The other night I ate at a real nice family restaurant. Every table had an argument going.

GEORGE CARLIN

DATE		

WHY I'M A LESS-THAN-PERFECT PARENT TODAY:

_____

_____

_____

_____

_____

_____

_____

_____

_____

_____

_____

_____

_____

_____

_____

_____

_____

_____

_____

_____

_____

_____

_____

_____

_____

_____

_____

TODAY'S PARENTAL SHORTCOMINGS INVOLVED:

Don't tell your kids you had an easy birth or they won't respect you. For years I used to wake up my daughter and say, "Melissa, you ripped me to shreds. Now go back to sleep."

JOAN RIVERS

	DATE	

WHY I'M A LESS-THAN-PERFECT PARENT TODAY:

_____
_____
_____
_____
_____
_____
_____
_____
_____
_____
_____
_____
_____
_____
_____
_____
_____
_____
_____
_____
_____
_____
_____
_____
_____
_____
_____

TODAY'S PARENTAL SHORTCOMINGS INVOLVED:

Children today are tyrants. They contradict their parents, gobble their food, and tyrannize their teachers.

SOCRATES

DATE

WHY I'M A LESS-THAN-PERFECT PARENT TODAY:

_____

_____

_____

_____

_____

_____

_____

_____

_____

_____

_____

_____

_____

_____

_____

_____

_____

_____

_____

_____

_____

_____

_____

_____

_____

_____

_____

_____

_____

_____

TODAY'S PARENTAL SHORTCOMINGS INVOLVED:

There is always some madness in love. But there is also always some reason in madness.

FRIEDRICH NIETZSCHE

DATE		

WHY I'M A LESS-THAN-PERFECT PARENT TODAY:

_____

_____

_____

_____

_____

_____

_____

_____

_____

_____

_____

_____

_____

_____

_____

_____

_____

_____

_____

_____

_____

_____

_____

_____

_____

_____

_____

_____

_____

_____

TODAY'S PARENTAL SHORTCOMINGS INVOLVED:

The trouble with children is that they are not returnable.

QUENTIN CRISP

DATE		

WHY I'M A LESS-THAN-PERFECT PARENT TODAY:

_____

_____

_____

_____

_____

_____

_____

_____

_____

_____

_____

_____

_____

_____

_____

_____

_____

_____

_____

_____

_____

_____

_____

_____

_____

TODAY'S PARENTAL SHORTCOMINGS INVOLVED:

Being a parent is wanting to hug and strangle your kid at the same time.

BILL WATTERSON

	DATE	

WHY I'M A LESS-THAN-PERFECT PARENT TODAY:

_____
_____
_____
_____
_____
_____
_____
_____
_____
_____
_____
_____
_____
_____
_____
_____
_____
_____
_____
_____
_____
_____
_____
_____
_____
_____
_____
_____
_____

TODAY'S PARENTAL SHORTCOMINGS INVOLVED:

Patience, n. A minor form of despair, disguised as a virtue.

AMBROSE BIERCE

DATE		

WHY I'M A LESS-THAN-PERFECT PARENT TODAY:

_____
_____
_____
_____
_____
_____
_____
_____
_____
_____
_____
_____
_____
_____
_____
_____
_____
_____
_____
_____
_____
_____
_____
_____
_____
_____
_____
_____

TODAY'S PARENTAL SHORTCOMINGS INVOLVED:

With a parent, it's always guilt. You want to be there, but you kind of also want to be here.

HEATHER LOCKLEAR

DATE

WHY I'M A LESS-THAN-PERFECT PARENT TODAY:

_____
_____
_____
_____
_____
_____
_____
_____
_____
_____
_____
_____
_____
_____
_____
_____
_____
_____
_____
_____
_____
_____
_____
_____
_____
_____

TODAY'S PARENTAL SHORTCOMINGS INVOLVED:

The informality of family life is a blessed condition that allows us all to become our best while looking our worst.

MARGE KENNEDY

DATE		

WHY I'M A LESS-THAN-PERFECT PARENT TODAY:

_____

_____

_____

_____

_____

_____

_____

_____

_____

_____

_____

_____

_____

_____

_____

_____

_____

_____

_____

_____

_____

_____

_____

_____

_____

_____

_____

TODAY'S PARENTAL SHORTCOMINGS INVOLVED:

Your responsibility as a parent is not as great as you might imagine. You need not supply the world with the next conqueror of disease or a major motion-picture star. If your child simply grows up to be someone who does not use the word "collectible" as a noun, you can consider yourself an unqualified success.

FRAN LEBOWITZ

	DATE	

WHY I'M A LESS-THAN-PERFECT PARENT TODAY:

_____

_____

_____

_____

_____

_____

_____

_____

_____

_____

_____

_____

_____

_____

_____

_____

_____

_____

_____

_____

_____

_____

_____

_____

_____

_____

_____

_____

_____

TODAY'S PARENTAL SHORTCOMINGS INVOLVED:

Teach your child to hold his tongue, he'll learn fast enough to speak.

BENJAMIN FRANKLIN

WHY I'M A LESS-THAN-PERFECT PARENT TODAY:

_____
_____
_____
_____
_____
_____
_____
_____
_____
_____
_____
_____
_____
_____
_____
_____
_____
_____
_____
_____
_____
_____
_____
_____
_____
_____
_____
_____
_____

TODAY'S PARENTAL SHORTCOMINGS INVOLVED:

When I was a boy, just about every summer we'd take a vacation. And you know, in eighteen years, we never had fun.

JOHN HUGHES

DATE

WHY I'M A LESS-THAN-PERFECT PARENT TODAY:

_____

_____

_____

_____

_____

_____

_____

_____

_____

_____

_____

_____

_____

_____

_____

_____

_____

_____

_____

_____

_____

_____

_____

_____

_____

_____

TODAY'S PARENTAL SHORTCOMINGS INVOLVED:

The truth is that parents are not really interested in justice. They just want quiet.

BILL COSBY

DATE		

WHY I'M A LESS-THAN-PERFECT PARENT TODAY:

_____

_____

_____

_____

_____

_____

_____

_____

_____

_____

_____

_____

_____

_____

_____

_____

_____

_____

_____

_____

_____

_____

TODAY'S PARENTAL SHORTCOMINGS INVOLVED:

Children can be awe-inspiringly horrible; manipulative, aggressive, rude, and unfeeling to a point where I often think that, if armed, they would make up the most terrifying fighting force the world has ever seen.

JILL TWEEDIE

DATE		

WHY I'M A LESS-THAN-PERFECT PARENT TODAY:

_____
_____
_____
_____
_____
_____
_____
_____
_____
_____
_____
_____
_____
_____
_____
_____
_____
_____
_____
_____
_____
_____
_____
_____
_____
_____

TODAY'S PARENTAL SHORTCOMINGS INVOLVED:

When my kids become wild and unruly, I use a nice, safe playpen. When they're finished, I climb out.

ERMA BOMBECK

DATE		

WHY I'M A LESS-THAN-PERFECT PARENT TODAY:

_____

_____

_____

_____

_____

_____

_____

_____

_____

_____

_____

_____

_____

_____

_____

_____

_____

_____

_____

_____

_____

_____

_____

_____

_____

_____

_____

TODAY'S PARENTAL SHORTCOMINGS INVOLVED:

Parents are the bones on which children sharpen their teeth.

PETER USTINOV

DATE

WHY I'M A LESS-THAN-PERFECT PARENT TODAY:

_____
_____
_____
_____
_____
_____
_____
_____
_____
_____
_____
_____
_____
_____
_____
_____
_____
_____
_____
_____
_____
_____
_____
_____
_____

TODAY'S PARENTAL SHORTCOMINGS INVOLVED:

We spend the first twelve months of our children's lives teaching them to walk and talk and the next twelve telling them to sit down and shut up.

PHYLLIS DILLER

DATE

WHY I'M A LESS-THAN-PERFECT PARENT TODAY:

_____

_____

_____

_____

_____

_____

_____

_____

_____

_____

_____

_____

_____

_____

_____

_____

_____

_____

_____

_____

_____

_____

_____

_____

TODAY'S PARENTAL SHORTCOMINGS INVOLVED:

Mother Nature, in her infinite wisdom, has instilled within each of us a powerful biological instinct to reproduce; this is her way of assuring that the human race, come what may, will never have any disposable income.

DAVE BARRY

DATE		

WHY I'M A LESS-THAN-PERFECT PARENT TODAY:

_____

_____

_____

_____

_____

_____

_____

_____

_____

_____

_____

_____

_____

_____

_____

_____

_____

_____

_____

_____

_____

_____

_____

_____

_____

_____

_____

TODAY'S PARENTAL SHORTCOMINGS INVOLVED:

I don't know any parents that look into the eyes of a newborn baby and say, "How can we screw this kid up?"

RUSSELL BISHOP

DATE		

WHY I'M A LESS-THAN-PERFECT PARENT TODAY:

_____
_____
_____
_____
_____
_____
_____
_____
_____
_____
_____
_____
_____
_____
_____
_____
_____
_____
_____
_____
_____
_____
_____
_____
_____
_____
_____
_____
_____

TODAY'S PARENTAL SHORTCOMINGS INVOLVED:

There are only two things a child will share willingly— communicable diseases and his mother's age.

DR. BENJAMIN SPOCK

WHY I'M A LESS-THAN-PERFECT PARENT TODAY:

_____

_____

_____

_____

_____

_____

_____

_____

_____

_____

_____

_____

_____

_____

_____

_____

_____

_____

_____

_____

_____

_____

_____

_____

_____

_____

_____

TODAY'S PARENTAL SHORTCOMINGS INVOLVED:

It kills you to see them grow up. But I guess it would kill you quicker if they didn't.

BARBARA KINGSOLVER

DATE	

WHY I'M A LESS-THAN-PERFECT PARENT TODAY:

_____

_____

_____

_____

_____

_____

_____

_____

_____

_____

_____

_____

_____

_____

_____

_____

_____

_____

_____

_____

_____

_____

_____

_____

TODAY'S PARENTAL SHORTCOMINGS INVOLVED:

I don't really know what to discipline my kids about because I don't think there's anything wrong with them. My son does outrageous things like taking his pants off at the table, and I know I should object but I find them so amusing. Maybe I'm making monsters of them but I can't help myself.

————————

UMA THURMAN

WHY I'M A LESS-THAN-PERFECT PARENT TODAY:

_____
_____
_____
_____
_____
_____
_____
_____
_____
_____
_____
_____
_____
_____
_____
_____
_____
_____
_____
_____
_____
_____
_____
_____
_____
_____
_____
_____
_____
_____

TODAY'S PARENTAL SHORTCOMINGS INVOLVED:

Children are given us to discourage our better emotions.

— **SAKI**

WHY I'M A LESS-THAN-PERFECT PARENT TODAY:

_____

_____

_____

_____

_____

_____

_____

_____

_____

_____

_____

_____

_____

_____

_____

_____

_____

_____

_____

_____

_____

_____

_____

_____

_____

_____

_____

TODAY'S PARENTAL SHORTCOMINGS INVOLVED:

Labor Day is a glorious holiday because your child will be going back to school the next day. It would have been called Independence Day, but that name was already taken.

BILL DODDS

DATE		

WHY I'M A LESS-THAN-PERFECT PARENT TODAY:

_____
_____
_____
_____
_____
_____
_____
_____
_____
_____
_____
_____
_____
_____
_____
_____
_____
_____
_____
_____
_____
_____
_____
_____
_____
_____
_____

TODAY'S PARENTAL SHORTCOMINGS INVOLVED:

It's frightening to think that you mark your children merely by being yourself . . . It seems unfair. You can't assume the responsibility for everything you do—or don't do.

SIMONE DE BEAUVOIR

WHY I'M A LESS-THAN-PERFECT PARENT TODAY:

_____
_____
_____
_____
_____
_____
_____
_____
_____
_____
_____
_____
_____
_____
_____
_____
_____
_____
_____
_____
_____
_____
_____
_____
_____
_____

TODAY'S PARENTAL SHORTCOMINGS INVOLVED:

Having a kid is great ... as long as his eyes are closed and he's not moving or speaking.

ADAM SANDLER

WHY I'M A LESS-THAN-PERFECT PARENT TODAY:

_____

_____

_____

_____

_____

_____

_____

_____

_____

_____

_____

_____

_____

_____

_____

_____

_____

_____

_____

_____

_____

_____

_____

_____

_____

TODAY'S PARENTAL SHORTCOMINGS INVOLVED:

A family is a unit composed not only of children but of men, women, an occasional animal, and the common cold.

OGDEN NASH

WHY I'M A LESS-THAN-PERFECT PARENT TODAY:

_____

_____

_____

_____

_____

_____

_____

_____

_____

_____

_____

_____

_____

_____

_____

_____

_____

_____

_____

_____

_____

_____

_____

_____

_____

_____

_____

_____

TODAY'S PARENTAL SHORTCOMINGS INVOLVED:

Sometimes I lie awake at night, and I ask, "Where have I gone wrong?" Then a voice says to me, "This is going to take more than one night."

CHARLES M. SCHULZ

WHY I'M A LESS-THAN-PERFECT PARENT TODAY:

_____

_____

_____

_____

_____

_____

_____

_____

_____

_____

_____

_____

_____

_____

_____

_____

_____

_____

_____

_____

_____

_____

_____

_____

TODAY'S PARENTAL SHORTCOMINGS INVOLVED:

The first half of our life is ruined by our parents and the second half by our children.

CLARENCE DARROW

WHY I'M A LESS-THAN-PERFECT PARENT TODAY:

_____

_____

_____

_____

_____

_____

_____

_____

_____

_____

_____

_____

_____

_____

_____

_____

_____

_____

_____

_____

_____

_____

_____

_____

_____

_____

TODAY'S PARENTAL SHORTCOMINGS INVOLVED:

Families are about love overcoming emotional torture.

MATT GROENING

WHY I'M A LESS-THAN-PERFECT PARENT TODAY:

_____

_____

_____

_____

_____

_____

_____

_____

_____

_____

_____

_____

_____

_____

_____

_____

_____

_____

_____

_____

_____

_____

_____

_____

_____

_____

_____

_____

TODAY'S PARENTAL SHORTCOMINGS INVOLVED:

The better you are as a parent, the richer the nest you've built, the more difficult it is for your kids to leave. So they have to invent things to dislike about you. And they're brilliant at it.

DUSTIN HOFFMAN

WHY I'M A LESS-THAN-PERFECT PARENT TODAY:

_____

_____

_____

_____

_____

_____

_____

_____

_____

_____

_____

_____

_____

_____

_____

_____

_____

_____

_____

_____

_____

_____

_____

_____

_____

_____

_____

_____

TODAY'S PARENTAL SHORTCOMINGS INVOLVED:

If you must hold yourself up to your children as an object lesson (which is not at all necessary), hold yourself up as a warning and not as an example.

GEORGE BERNARD SHAW

DATE		

WHY I'M A LESS-THAN-PERFECT PARENT TODAY:

_____

_____

_____

_____

_____

_____

_____

_____

_____

_____

_____

_____

_____

_____

_____

_____

_____

_____

_____

_____

_____

_____

_____

_____

_____

_____

_____

TODAY'S PARENTAL SHORTCOMINGS INVOLVED:

Like all parents, my husband and I just do the best we can, and hold our breath, and hope we've set aside enough money to pay for our kids' therapy.

MICHELLE PFEIFFER

DATE		

WHY I'M A LESS-THAN-PERFECT PARENT TODAY:

_____

_____

_____

_____

_____

_____

_____

_____

_____

_____

_____

_____

_____

_____

_____

_____

_____

_____

_____

_____

_____

_____

_____

_____

_____

TODAY'S PARENTAL SHORTCOMINGS INVOLVED:

People talk about "dysfunctional" families;
I've never seen any other kind.

SUE GRAFTON

WHY I'M A LESS-THAN-PERFECT PARENT TODAY:

_____

_____

_____

_____

_____

_____

_____

_____

_____

_____

_____

_____

_____

_____

_____

_____

_____

_____

_____

_____

_____

_____

_____

_____

_____

_____

_____

_____

_____

TODAY'S PARENTAL SHORTCOMINGS INVOLVED:

Sometimes when I look at all my children, I say to myself, "Lillian, you should have stayed a virgin."

LILLIAN CARTER

WHY I'M A LESS-THAN-PERFECT PARENT TODAY:

_____

_____

_____

_____

_____

_____

_____

_____

_____

_____

_____

_____

_____

_____

_____

_____

_____

_____

_____

_____

_____

_____

_____

_____

_____

TODAY'S PARENTAL SHORTCOMINGS INVOLVED:

If you want to recapture your youth, just cut off his allowance.

AL BERNSTEIN

DATE		

WHY I'M A LESS-THAN-PERFECT PARENT TODAY:

_____

_____

_____

_____

_____

_____

_____

_____

_____

_____

_____

_____

_____

_____

_____

_____

_____

_____

_____

_____

_____

_____

_____

_____

_____

_____

_____

_____

_____

_____

TODAY'S PARENTAL SHORTCOMINGS INVOLVED:

Children from the age of five to ten should watch more television. Television depicts adults as rotten SOBs, given to fistfights, gunplay, and other mayhem. Kids who believe this about grown-ups aren't likely to argue about bedtime.

P. J. O'ROURKE

DATE		

WHY I'M A LESS-THAN-PERFECT PARENT TODAY:

_____

_____

_____

_____

_____

_____

_____

_____

_____

_____

_____

_____

_____

_____

_____

_____

_____

_____

_____

_____

_____

_____

_____

_____

_____

TODAY'S PARENTAL SHORTCOMINGS INVOLVED:

Few misfortunes can befall a boy which bring worse consequences than to have a really affectionate mother.

W. SOMERSET MAUGHAM

DATE

WHY I'M A LESS-THAN-PERFECT PARENT TODAY:

_____

_____

_____

_____

_____

_____

_____

_____

_____

_____

_____

_____

_____

_____

_____

_____

_____

_____

_____

_____

_____

_____

_____

_____

_____

_____

TODAY'S PARENTAL SHORTCOMINGS INVOLVED:

Of children as of
procreation—the
pleasure momentary,
the posture ridiculous,
the expense damnable.

EVELYN WAUGH

DATE

WHY I'M A LESS-THAN-PERFECT PARENT TODAY:

_____

_____

_____

_____

_____

_____

_____

_____

_____

_____

_____

_____

_____

_____

_____

_____

_____

_____

_____

_____

_____

_____

_____

_____

_____

_____

TODAY'S PARENTAL SHORTCOMINGS INVOLVED:

The one thing I never feel secure about is the way I parent.

TERI HATCHER

WHY I'M A LESS-THAN-PERFECT PARENT TODAY:

TODAY'S PARENTAL SHORTCOMINGS INVOLVED:

Children are like aliens—they might as well have antennas.

KATHY GRIFFIN

DATE		

WHY I'M A LESS-THAN-PERFECT PARENT TODAY:

_____

_____

_____

_____

_____

_____

_____

_____

_____

_____

_____

_____

_____

_____

_____

_____

_____

_____

_____

_____

_____

_____

_____

_____

TODAY'S PARENTAL SHORTCOMINGS INVOLVED:

You will find as the children grow up that as a rule children are a bitter disappointment— their greatest object being to do precisely what their parents do not wish and have anxiously tried to prevent.

QUEEN VICTORIA

DATE		

WHY I'M A LESS-THAN-PERFECT PARENT TODAY:

_____

_____

_____

_____

_____

_____

_____

_____

_____

_____

_____

_____

_____

_____

_____

_____

_____

_____

_____

_____

_____

_____

_____

_____

_____

_____

_____

_____

TODAY'S PARENTAL SHORTCOMINGS INVOLVED:

I think a dysfunctional
family is any family
with more than one
person in it.

_____

JERRY SEINFELD

WHY I'M A LESS-THAN-PERFECT PARENT TODAY:

TODAY'S PARENTAL SHORTCOMINGS INVOLVED:

Ask your child what
he wants for dinner
only if he's buying.

FRAN LEBOWITZ

WHY I'M A LESS-THAN-PERFECT PARENT TODAY:

_____

_____

_____

_____

_____

_____

_____

_____

_____

_____

_____

_____

_____

_____

_____

_____

_____

_____

_____

_____

_____

_____

_____

_____

_____

_____

TODAY'S PARENTAL SHORTCOMINGS INVOLVED:

There are times when parenthood seems nothing but feeding the mouth that bites you.

PETER DE VRIES

DATE		

WHY I'M A LESS-THAN-PERFECT PARENT TODAY:

TODAY'S PARENTAL SHORTCOMINGS INVOLVED:

I love my children ... I'm delighted to see them come and delighted to see them go.

MARY WESLEY

DATE

WHY I'M A LESS-THAN-PERFECT PARENT TODAY:

TODAY'S PARENTAL SHORTCOMINGS INVOLVED:

No matter how calmly you try to referee, parenting will eventually produce bizarre behavior, and I'm not talking about the kids.

BILL COSBY

WHY I'M A LESS-THAN-PERFECT PARENT TODAY:

_____

_____

_____

_____

_____

_____

_____

_____

_____

_____

_____

_____

_____

_____

_____

_____

_____

_____

_____

_____

_____

_____

_____

_____

_____

_____

TODAY'S PARENTAL SHORTCOMINGS INVOLVED:

The pressures of being a parent are equal to any pressure on earth. To be a conscious parent, and really look to that little being's mental and physical health, is a responsibility which most of us, including me, avoid most of the time, because it's too hard. To put it loosely, the reason why kids are crazy is because nobody can face the responsibility of bringing them up.

JOHN LENNON

WHY I'M A LESS-THAN-PERFECT PARENT TODAY:

TODAY'S PARENTAL SHORTCOMINGS INVOLVED:

There are three terrible ages of childhood— one to ten, ten to twenty, and twenty to thirty.

CLEVELAND AMORY

WHY I'M A LESS-THAN-PERFECT PARENT TODAY:

_____

_____

_____

_____

_____

_____

_____

_____

_____

_____

_____

_____

_____

_____

_____

_____

_____

_____

_____

_____

_____

_____

_____

_____

_____

_____

_____

_____

TODAY'S PARENTAL SHORTCOMINGS INVOLVED:

Children begin by loving their parents;
after a time they judge them; rarely,
if ever, do they forgive them.

OSCAR WILDE

WHY I'M A LESS-THAN-PERFECT PARENT TODAY:

_____

_____

_____

_____

_____

_____

_____

_____

_____

_____

_____

_____

_____

_____

_____

_____

_____

_____

_____

_____

_____

_____

_____

_____

_____

_____

_____

TODAY'S PARENTAL SHORTCOMINGS INVOLVED:

As a child my family's menu consisted of two choices: take it or leave it.

BUDDY HACKETT

DATE		

WHY I'M A LESS-THAN-PERFECT PARENT TODAY:

_____
_____
_____
_____
_____
_____
_____
_____
_____
_____
_____
_____
_____
_____
_____
_____
_____
_____
_____
_____
_____
_____
_____
_____
_____
_____

TODAY'S PARENTAL SHORTCOMINGS INVOLVED:

Insanity is hereditary; you can get it from your children.

SAM LEVENSON

DATE

WHY I'M A LESS-THAN-PERFECT PARENT TODAY:

_____

_____

_____

_____

_____

_____

_____

_____

_____

_____

_____

_____

_____

_____

_____

_____

_____

_____

_____

_____

_____

_____

_____

_____

_____

TODAY'S PARENTAL SHORTCOMINGS INVOLVED:

Before I got married I had six theories about bringing up children; now I have six children and no theories.

JOHN WILMOT

WHY I'M A LESS-THAN-PERFECT PARENT TODAY:

_____

_____

_____

_____

_____

_____

_____

_____

_____

_____

_____

_____

_____

_____

_____

_____

_____

_____

_____

_____

_____

_____

_____

_____

_____

_____

_____

_____

_____

TODAY'S PARENTAL SHORTCOMINGS INVOLVED:

We're more interesting if we are dysfunctional.

RUPERT EVERETT

DATE

WHY I'M A LESS-THAN-PERFECT PARENT TODAY:

_____

_____

_____

_____

_____

_____

_____

_____

_____

_____

_____

_____

_____

_____

_____

_____

_____

_____

_____

_____

_____

_____

_____

_____

TODAY'S PARENTAL SHORTCOMINGS INVOLVED:

The best way to keep children at home is to make the home atmosphere pleasant— and let the air out of the tires.

DOROTHY PARKER

WHY I'M A LESS-THAN-PERFECT PARENT TODAY:

_____
_____
_____
_____
_____
_____
_____
_____
_____
_____
_____
_____
_____
_____
_____
_____
_____
_____
_____
_____
_____
_____
_____
_____

TODAY'S PARENTAL SHORTCOMINGS INVOLVED:

Raising kids is part joy and part guerrilla warfare.

ED ASNER

WHY I'M A LESS-THAN-PERFECT PARENT TODAY:

_____

_____

_____

_____

_____

_____

_____

_____

_____

_____

_____

_____

_____

_____

_____

_____

_____

_____

_____

_____

_____

_____

_____

_____

_____

_____

_____

TODAY'S PARENTAL SHORTCOMINGS INVOLVED:

Everyone should have kids. They are the greatest joy in the world. But they are also terrorists. You'll realize this as soon as they are born and they start using sleep deprivation to break you.

RAY ROMANO

WHY I'M A LESS-THAN-PERFECT PARENT TODAY:

TODAY'S PARENTAL SHORTCOMINGS INVOLVED:

Don't try to make children grow up to be like you, or they may do it.

RUSSELL BAKER

WHY I'M A LESS-THAN-PERFECT PARENT TODAY:

_____

_____

_____

_____

_____

_____

_____

_____

_____

_____

_____

_____

_____

_____

_____

_____

_____

_____

_____

_____

_____

_____

_____

_____

TODAY'S PARENTAL SHORTCOMINGS INVOLVED:

I never really believed it before, but when you have a child, there really aren't enough hours in the day to do anything. I had to go for a dental checkup the other day and they were going, "Can you floss and then rub your gums with this?," and I was thinking, "Are you serious? It's just not going to happen."

TINA FEY

DATE

WHY I'M A LESS-THAN-PERFECT PARENT TODAY:

_____

_____

_____

_____

_____

_____

_____

_____

_____

_____

_____

_____

_____

_____

_____

_____

_____

_____

_____

_____

_____

_____

_____

_____

_____

_____

_____

TODAY'S PARENTAL SHORTCOMINGS INVOLVED:

Now the thing about
having a baby—and I
can't be the first person
to have noticed this—
is that thereafter you
have it.

JEAN KERR

WHY I'M A LESS-THAN-PERFECT PARENT TODAY:

_____
_____
_____
_____
_____
_____
_____
_____
_____
_____
_____
_____
_____
_____
_____
_____
_____
_____
_____
_____
_____
_____
_____
_____
_____
_____
_____
_____
_____
_____

TODAY'S PARENTAL SHORTCOMINGS INVOLVED:

Children aren't happy
  with nothing to ignore,
And that's what parents
  were created for.

OGDEN NASH

WHY I'M A LESS-THAN-PERFECT PARENT TODAY:

_____
_____
_____
_____
_____
_____
_____
_____
_____
_____
_____
_____
_____
_____
_____
_____
_____
_____
_____
_____
_____
_____
_____
_____

TODAY'S PARENTAL SHORTCOMINGS INVOLVED:

I figure that if the children are alive when I get home, I've done my job.

ROSEANNE BARR

WHY I'M A LESS-THAN-PERFECT PARENT TODAY:

_____
_____
_____
_____
_____
_____
_____
_____
_____
_____
_____
_____
_____
_____
_____
_____
_____
_____
_____
_____
_____
_____
_____
_____
_____
_____
_____
_____
_____
_____
_____

TODAY'S PARENTAL SHORTCOMINGS INVOLVED:

If Mr. Vincent Price were to be co-starred
with Miss Bette Davis in a story by Mr. Edgar
Allan Poe directed by Mr. Roger Corman,
it could not fully express the pent-up violence
and depravity of a single day in the life of the
average family.

QUENTIN CRISP

WHY I'M A LESS-THAN-PERFECT PARENT TODAY:

_____

_____

_____

_____

_____

_____

_____

_____

_____

_____

_____

_____

_____

_____

_____

_____

_____

_____

_____

_____

_____

_____

_____

_____

TODAY'S PARENTAL SHORTCOMINGS INVOLVED:

I believe that we parents must encourage our children to become educated, so they can get into a good college that we cannot afford.

DAVE BARRY

DATE		

WHY I'M A LESS-THAN-PERFECT PARENT TODAY:

_____

_____

_____

_____

_____

_____

_____

_____

_____

_____

_____

_____

_____

_____

_____

_____

_____

_____

_____

_____

_____

_____

_____

_____

_____

_____

_____

TODAY'S PARENTAL SHORTCOMINGS INVOLVED:

At some point we run out of lyrics to
the lullabies and start singing,
"Hush little baby, don't be contrary,
Mama's gonna have a coro-nary."

BARBARA KINGSOLVER

WHY I'M A LESS-THAN-PERFECT PARENT TODAY:

_____
_____
_____
_____
_____
_____
_____
_____
_____
_____
_____
_____
_____
_____
_____
_____
_____
_____
_____
_____
_____
_____
_____
_____
_____

TODAY'S PARENTAL SHORTCOMINGS INVOLVED:

What you discovered
about yourself in raising
children wasn't always
agreeable or attractive.

JONATHAN FRANZEN

DATE		

WHY I'M A LESS-THAN-PERFECT PARENT TODAY:

_____

_____

_____

_____

_____

_____

_____

_____

_____

_____

_____

_____

_____

_____

_____

_____

_____

_____

_____

_____

_____

_____

_____

_____

_____

TODAY'S PARENTAL SHORTCOMINGS INVOLVED:

Kids are the best ... You can teach them to hate the things you hate. And they practically raise themselves, what with the Internet and all.

MATT GROENING

WHY I'M A LESS-THAN-PERFECT PARENT TODAY:

_____

_____

_____

_____

_____

_____

_____

_____

_____

_____

_____

_____

_____

_____

_____

_____

_____

_____

_____

_____

_____

_____

_____

_____

_____

_____

_____

_____

TODAY'S PARENTAL SHORTCOMINGS INVOLVED:

Most children threaten at times to run away from home. This is the only thing that keeps some parents going.

PHYLLIS DILLER

WHY I'M A LESS-THAN-PERFECT PARENT TODAY:

_____
_____
_____
_____
_____
_____
_____
_____
_____
_____
_____
_____
_____
_____
_____
_____
_____
_____
_____
_____
_____
_____
_____
_____
_____
_____
_____

TODAY'S PARENTAL SHORTCOMINGS INVOLVED:

A child is a curly, dimpled lunatic.

RALPH WALDO EMERSON

WHY I'M A LESS-THAN-PERFECT PARENT TODAY:

_____

_____

_____

_____

_____

_____

_____

_____

_____

_____

_____

_____

_____

_____

_____

_____

_____

_____

_____

_____

_____

_____

TODAY'S PARENTAL SHORTCOMINGS INVOLVED:

Tired is the new black.

AMY POEHLER

DATE

WHY I'M A LESS-THAN-PERFECT PARENT TODAY:

_____

_____

_____

_____

_____

_____

_____

_____

_____

_____

_____

_____

_____

_____

_____

_____

_____

_____

_____

_____

_____

_____

_____

_____

_____

TODAY'S PARENTAL SHORTCOMINGS INVOLVED:

What is a home without children? Quiet.

HENNY YOUNGMAN

WHY I'M A LESS-THAN-PERFECT PARENT TODAY:

TODAY'S PARENTAL SHORTCOMINGS INVOLVED:

You're doing better than you think.

———

KNOCK KNOCK